W9-AXF-179

# WINNERS
# IN
# GYMNASTICS

FRANK LITSKY has been a sports writer and editor for thirty-two years. He has written books for young readers as well as for adults. He is currently the assistant sports editor for The New York Times.

# WINNERS
## IN
# GYMNASTICS

BY FRANK LITSKY

AN AVON CAMELOT BOOK

Cover photo of Nadia Comaneci by DUOMO/Paul J. Sutton.

Other photos by DUOMO/Paul J. Sutton: pp. 10, 13, 24, 35, and 39; DUOMO/Steve E. Sutton: pp. 20 and 36; DUOMO/Gale Constable: p. 44; George Kalinsky: pp. 19, 23, 32, 40, and 43; A.F.P. from Pictorial Parade: p. 16; Tyrone Dukes/The New York Times: p. 47.

AVON BOOKS
A division of
The Hearst Corporation
959 Eighth Avenue
New York, New York 10019

Copyright © 1978 by Frank Litsky
Published by arrangement with Franklin Watts, Inc.
Library of Congress Catalog Card Number: 77-17535
ISBN: 0-380-43299-4

All rights reserved, which includes the right
to reproduce this book or portions thereof in
any form whatsoever. For information address
Franklin Watts, Inc.,
730 Fifth Avenue, New York, New York 10019

First Avon Printing, April, 1979
Second Printing

AVON TRADEMARK REG. U.S. PAT. OFF. AND IN
OTHER COUNTRIES, MARCA REGISTRADA, HECHO EN
U.S.A.

Printed in the U.S.A.

# CONTENTS

# INTRODUCTION

Gymnastic sports were first played in ancient Greece. Then they almost disappeared for nearly 2,000 years. Now people all over the world are doing them again. Male and female gymnasts perform in national and world competitions, or contests. Gymnastics are a popular part of the Olympic Games, too. Almost every country in the world sends gymnasts to compete. Each gymnast represents his or her country.

In gymnastic competition, men compete against men. Women compete against women. There are six individual events for men. There are four for women. There are also team events.

After performing an event, the gymnast receives a score. There are four judges. Each gives the gymnast up to 10 points. A score of around 9 is very good. A perfect score of 10 is rare. The scores are all added up. The gymnast with the highest score wins the event. There is also an all-round champion.

The winners of large competitions receive medals. First place earns a gold medal. Second place gets a silver medal. Third place wins a bronze medal.

Being strong is important for all gymnasts. So is being graceful. But for men, strength is more important. For women, grace is more important.

The only event both men and women do is the floor exercise. But women do it to music. The other men's events are:

1. the horizontal bar
2. the parallel bars
3. the long horse vault
4. the still rings
5. the pommeled horse (also called the side horse)

The other women's events are:
1. the uneven parallel bars
2. the balance beam
3. the side horse vault

These events are named for the equipment used while performing.

Now let's find out about some winners in gymnastics!

# NADIA COMANECI

Only the best gymnasts compete in the
Olympics. The 1976 Olympics were held
in Montreal, Canada. Nadia Comaneci
(NAH-dee-ah koh-mah-NEECH) was in
all the women's events. Nadia is from
Onesti, Rumania. Rumania is a country
in Eastern Europe. She was only 14
years old at the time. She stood 4 feet
11 inches (1.50 m) tall. She weighed
86 pounds (39 kg). She looked like a
Barbi doll. But she thrilled television
audiences everywhere with her
performances.

Nadia won three gold medals in
the Olympics. She also won a bronze
medal. But more important, she did
something never done before. No
gymnast had ever scored a 10 in the
Olympics. This is a perfect score. Nadia

scored seven 10s. Afterward, she was voted the best female athlete in the world. This includes all sports.

Nadia was born in 1961. She started gymnastics when she was 6. One day she was playing in the schoolyard with her friend. It was recess. A gymnastics coach named Bela Karolyi saw the girls. He thought they could both become good gymnasts. He wanted to talk to them. But at that moment the bell rang. The girls ran inside.

The coach tried to find them. He looked in every room and failed. He

Nadia Comaneci doing
her famous routine
on the balance beam.

tried again. He failed again. Then he went back a third time. This time he asked, "Who likes gymnastics?" Finally, in one room, two girls jumped up. They shouted, "We do! We do!" The two girls were Nadia and her friend.

The coach put the girls through a test. He watched them run. He watched them jump. Then he had them walk on a balance beam. The beam is only 4 inches (10 cm) wide. It is 16 feet (4.87 m) long and 4 feet (1.22 m) off the ground. Many people are afraid to walk on it. Not Nadia. She loved it.

The coach was now sure both girls were very talented. He was right.

Nadia accepting the gold medal for the balance beam event. On Nadia's right is Olga Korbut.

Nadia's friend became a ballerina. Nadia became a great gymnast.

When Nadia was 7, she entered the Rumanian junior championships. She finished thirteenth. When she was 8, she won the junior championships. When she was 13, she won the women's European championship. She beat many famous gymnasts from other countries. Gymnastic fans now knew who Nadia was. But after the 1976 Olympics, the world knew. Nadia was the best.

Nadia's father is a car mechanic. Her mother works in an office. Nadia has a brother, Adrian. He is four years younger than she.

Being the world's best gymnast isn't good enough for Nadia. She says, "Now I would like to do better than before." And she probably will.

# OLGA KORBUT

Until Nadia, the world's most famous gymnast was Olga Korbut. Olga was born in 1955. She comes from a city in Russia named Grodno. Like most gymnasts, Olga is tiny. But she has a big smile.

Before Olga, not many people knew of gymnastics.

The 1972 Olympics were held in Munich, Germany. Olga was 17 at the time. She had been performing well. Her enthusiasm won over the crowds. Then she made two bad mistakes. Olga was performing on the uneven parallel bars. Her feet touched the floor. They weren't supposed to. A moment later, her hand slipped from the bar. She bravely finished her routine. But then, right on television, she cried.

The next day, Olga was back. This time, she was almost perfect. She won three gold medals and one silver medal.

Before Olga, not many girls trained in gymnastics. Now, hundreds of thousands do. This is thanks to Olga. During 1973 and 1974, Olga and her teammates performed in many cities. Wherever they went, every seat was filled. Everyone wanted to see Olga.

Olga always liked to try new things in gymnastics. She once did a back somersault on the balance beam. No one had ever done this before. She also did a half back somersault on the uneven parallel bars. No one had done

Olga Korbut showing
the gold medal she won
in the 1972 Olympics.

this before either. The judges were afraid she would get hurt. They wanted to stop her from doing them. But Olga said she wasn't afraid. She also said she'd quit gymnastics if they stopped her. So they let her keep on. Soon, other gymnasts were doing these moves, too.

In 1976, Olga won only one Olympic medal. It was a silver one. She won it for her performance on the balance beam. Nadia Comaneci won the gold in this event. On the victory stand, the two stood together. They were given their medals. Nadia had been more perfect. But Olga got the biggest cheers. She was still the most popular.

Olga on the balance beam.

The 1976 Russian women's team
with its Olympic gold medals.

(20)

# NELLI KIM

All gymnasts are graceful. Nelli Kim
may be the most graceful. She is
certainly the best Russian female
gymnast. She moves more smoothly
than most other gymnasts. Her body
seems to flow.

Nelli was born in 1957 in the town
of Chemkent. Chemkent is near the city
of Leningrad. Nelli's father is half-
Korean. He works in a roofing factory.

When Nelli was 9, a gymnastics
coach noticed her. He thought she was
especially graceful. He had her sent to
a special sports school for girls. The
school was in her home town. There
she learned gymnastics. The girls in
the school came from all over Russia.
They were all good at gymnastics. Every
morning, Nelli and her schoolmates

would study regular subjects. In the afternoon they would study gymnastics. The coaches would explain what to do. Then the girls would train for hours.

The best girls stayed in the school for many years. The others were sent home. They would go back to regular schools. Nelli stayed on.

At 16, Nelli entered her first world competition. She placed third on the balance beam. At 17, she won a silver medal in the European championships. But other Russian girls were doing better. So no one expected what happened next. In 1976, Nelli won three Olympic gold medals. One was for her floor exercises. Many gymnasts seem

Nelli Kim, the best in the world in floor exercises.

too serious. Not Nelli. She looks like she's having fun. This is especially true when she's doing floor exercises. When Nelli does them, she looks as if she's dancing.

Nelli also won a gold for the vault event. And her team won the team championship. So her third gold was for being on the Russian team.

When everything goes right, Nelli can be great. She had two perfect scores of 10 in the Olympics. But in another event, she fell off the bars. She hardly seemed upset. She said it

Nelli enjoying the crowd's applause. She has just received the gold medal in the 1976 Olympics. On her left is Ludmilla Turisheva. Ludmilla is another brilliant Russian gymnast.

happened because she was trying too hard. She was trying to do too much.

Nelli spends a lot of time away from home. In 1976 she spent two months at a sports school in Moscow. She spent seven months competing. Nelli doesn't like this part of gymnastics. She also finds the training very hard. In competition, a gymnast spends only 90 seconds on the beam. Only 23 seconds are spent on the uneven parallel bars. But practice sessions can go on for many hours.

Nelli used to spend five hours a day at practice. Her coaches enjoyed teaching her. They loved her personality. And she was able to do many difficult movements. But now Nelli trains only about an hour each day. She says she would rather listen to Stevie Wonder records.

# CATHY RIGBY MASON

In 1968, a young American gymnast performed in the Olympics. Her name was Cathy Rigby. She was only 15 years old. In fact, she was the youngest American athlete there that year. She came in sixteenth in the all-round gymnastic competition. This was the best any American woman gymnast had done.

Cathy was born in 1952. She grew up in Lakewood, California. She was always small for her age. At school, her classmates made fun of her. They said she looked too young to be in school. They told her, "Go home until you get bigger."

When Cathy was 10, she started gymnastics. Her coach was Bud Marquette. Bud said Cathy never showed any fear. In fact, she tried many moves on her own. Some were dangerous. In class, Bud often had to stop her. He wanted her to wait for the others.

Before she was 15, Cathy was working at gymnastics seven hours a day. At night she learned Spanish. She knew she was going to the Olympics in Mexico She wanted to be able to talk to the people there.

At 17, Cathy entered the world championships. They were held in Yugoslavia. Yugoslavia is in Eastern Europe. Cathy finished second on the balance beam. This was a first. No American woman before had won a medal in such an important

Cathy Rigby, America's best-ever woman gymnast on the balance beam.

competition. Cathy's picture appeared on magazine covers. Whenever she competed, the meet would be shown on television.

In 1972 Cathy again tried out for the Olympics. She was leading in the trials. Then she hurt her right foot. She couldn't finish. But she was put on the team anyway. Everyone knew she was the best American gymnast. She finished tenth in the all-round competition. No American woman has yet done better.

In 1973 Cathy married Tommy Mason. Tommy is an ex-football player. She stopped competing. Since then, she has played Peter Pan in the theater. She also often appears on televised gymnastic events. She explains the sport and the judges' scoring to viewers.

# NIKOLAI ANDRIANOV

Nikolai Andrianov (NEE-koh-lie AHN-dree-AH-nov) of Russia is the world's best male gymnast. He was born in 1952. He had three brothers and sisters. His mother worked. His father didn't live with them. Nikolai was always in trouble. He didn't do his homework. Teachers didn't like him. They sent notes home to his mother.

One day, a friend brought Nikolai to his gymnastics club. The coach there was Nikolai Polkachev. Polkachev had trouble with young Nikolai, too. The boy liked gymnastics and was good at it. But he kept getting into trouble. So the coach took Nikolai to live with him. Nikolai was 11 years old. Before long, he started doing better in school.

Boys usually start competing in gymnastics later than girls. They aren't strong enough until 13 or 14 years old. Nikolai entered his first competition at 17. By 18, he was on the Russian team.

Nikolai was the best Russian gymnast on the still rings. These require very strong arms. In fact, Nikolai was the strongest gymnast on the team. But he didn't always try hard. One time, he was first on the still rings. But he fell off the pommeled horse. Another time, he got an almost perfect score on the vault. Then he tripped doing his floor exercises. He was always making big mistakes.

Nikolai Andrianov's strength is important on the rings.

In 1972, Nikolai won an Olympic gold medal. He also won three gold medals in European championships. But he knew he could do even better. He started to work harder. He also got married. His wife is Lyubov Burda. She was a Russian gymnastics champion at 15. She knew how hard Nikolai would have to work. She helped him become more confident.

At the 1976 Olympics, Nikolai was at his best. The most medals he could have won was eight. He won seven. Four were gold. No other Olympic athlete won as many medals that year. For the first time, Nikolai didn't make mistakes.

Nikolai on the victory stand in the 1976 Olympics.

# MITSUO TSUKAHARA

Mitsuo Tsukahara (mit-SOO-oh soo-kah-HAR-ah) is from Tokyo (TOE-key-oh), Japan. He was born in 1947. He is old for a gymnast. He has already been in three Olympic competitions. But he says he feels stronger now than ever before. He also says he wants to compete for ten more years. He loves to travel and to compete.

There were no gymnastics in Japan before World War II. In 1948, three American gymnasts went to Japan. They taught the Japanese the sport. By 1956, Japan had an Olympic team. In the 1960 Olympics, their men's team was the best in the world.

Mitsuo Tsukahara's free exercise routine.

Mitsuo watched the 1960 Olympics on television. He was 12 years old. He had never seen gymnastics performed before. He thought they were beautiful. Right then, he decided to become a gymnast. He wanted to be an Olympic champion.

In five years, Mitsuo became Japan's best high school gymnast. Then, in 1966, he became a national champion. Since then, he has won eight Olympic medals. In the 1976 Olympics alone, he won five. Two were gold, one was silver, and two were bronze.

Mitsuo has given a lot to gymnastics. He has made up new moves. One is the "Tsukahara vault." This is a twisting somersault at the end

Mitsuo between the parallel bars in the 1976 Olympics.

of a vault. Many other gymnasts now use it. Nelli Kim used it in one event. She scored a perfect 10.

Tsukahara often works with youngsters. He would be a good coach. But he would rather compete.

Mitsuo works for a company that makes musical instruments. As a teen-ager, he trained five hours a day. Now he trains for only three. He says that is enough for his age.

Japan's most popular sports are baseball and wrestling. But Mitsuo is Japan's most popular athlete. Every day, people stop him on the street. Some want to talk to him about gymnastics. Others just want to thank him for bringing glory to Japan.

Mitsuo on the horizontal bar.

# BART CONNER

Bart Conner is America's best all-round male gymnast. He was born in 1958. He comes from Morton Grove, Illinois.

Everyone in Bart's house is an athlete. He has two brothers. His older brother is a speed skater. He almost made the 1976 Olympic team. His younger brother plays soccer at school.

As a youngster, Bart tried many sports. He was good at speed and figure skating. He liked tennis and golf. But he was too small for some sports. He was a good football player, for example. But only as long as the other players weren't too big.

Then, at 10, Bart tried gymnastics at

Bart Conner works out on the pommeled horse.

a YMCA. He found he could easily stand on his hands. He could also tumble. He began competing for the YMCA team soon after.

He wasn't really brave at first. Many things about gymnastics scared him. He was very careful. He didn't try anything too dangerous. As he got better, he became more confident. Then he tried new things.

Bart thinks his parents are very special. They wanted Bart to keep at gymnastics. But only if he wanted it. They told him he didn't have to struggle. But if he didn't, they said, he'd never be good. It was all up to him. Bart decided on his own to be a champion.

Bart about to start
his routine on the rings.

Bart always got good marks in school. At 17, he competed in his first national championships. He did very well. He became the all-round champion. On his eighteenth birthday, he won the American Cup. He beat some of the best gymnasts in the world. Among them were Nikolai Andrianov and Mitsuo Tsukahara. Now Bart was one of the best. He competed in the 1976 Olympics. He didn't win any medals. But his real dream is for the 1980 Olympics.

Bart's best events are the parallel bars and the pommeled horse. In these events, the arms stay close to the body. Bart can do this well. He has more difficulty on the still rings. For this,

Mitsuo, left, relaxing with
Bart Conner before a competition.

the arms must be out from the body. This requires greater strength. Bart is trying to get his arms stronger.

Bart is now a college student. He goes to the University of Oklahoma. Besides gymnastics, he likes to ski when he can. He enjoys many sports. But because he is small, he still likes gymnastics best. Small people can somersault very easily.